# FRONTISPIECE

This all began as an exercise in oral history by a WEA Local History Class meeting in Irby, Wirral, over a period of three years.

Our first efforts proved to be so successful that we thought others might be interested in our reminiscences too, so we ventured into publication.

Our thanks go to staff at Irby and Birkenhead Central Libraries, to Mr George Rawsthorne and WEA staff for professional advice and help.

Acknowledgements to Liverpool Daily Post & Echo and to Fox Photos Ltd, for use of photographs.

Class members who helped to compile this booklet include:—

Mrs I. Barker, Mr and Mrs W. Bunn, Mrs Carpenter, Mr and Mrs G. Dutton, Miss Potter, Mr and Mrs G. Rawsthorne, Mr and Mrs Gifford, Mr A. Stananought, Mrs D. Smith, Mr V. Torrens, Miss White, Mrs Williams and I. Bushell (Tutor).

When war broke out I was living in West Kirby and travelled by train every day to my job in a Liverpool bank. I have memories of a very friendly journey, on the steam trains. Wirral was much more rural then, and West Kirby beach was a very popular venue for day-trips. There were all the usual seaside attractions, tea-shops and bucket-and-spade shops near to the beach, also horse and trap rides out to Hilbre Island.

In the 'Phoney War' period in 1939, empty houses in West Kirby were taken over by important 'volunteer ladies' who organized the evacuation of children from Liverpool. (Children with skin diseases were put in a separate house). Later evacuees from Liverpool went to North Wales.

In October 1939 our wedding took place as planned (with our fingers crossed that nothing would go wrong). The reception took place at the bride's home, and we had the last iced wedding cake before restrictions were placed on sugar, etc. After that date, the confectioner would provide a cardboard cover for the cake made to look like icing, as no icing-sugar was available. There was also petrol rationing but this did not present much of a problem at the time as the allowance was fair. However, we were only allowed to travel within 30 miles from home for our honeymoon, and Identity Cards and Ration Books had to be carried; though we found these were not needed in Llangollen (our destination) as people lived well there and seemed unaffected by rationing or the war, even though all station and road signs had been removed and there was Blackout in operation.

After marriage we set up home in Wallasey, and I worked with the Red Cross Libraries at the Customs House in Liverpool, until the building was bombed, burnt out, and finally condemned. Later I worked in the Censorship building in Edge Lane, and was trained and paid for this work — the censoring of mail to America — which was covered by the Official Secrets Act.

While we were in Wallasey, the first bomb was dropped there at Stroud's Corner. There was no air-raid shelter in the garden so we were supposed to hide under the stairs for safety! We were near the river so could watch the German planes flying low over the dock area, taking reconaissance photos.

It was considered safer to sleep downstairs, and have our living rooms upstairs in case of bombing at night.

In 1941 my husband was called-up, so we gave up our home in Wallasey and put the furniture in store, while I returned to live with my parents in West Kirby, which was thought to be a safer place than

# Wirral at War

*Compiled by members of an Irby WEA Local History Class*

First published 1991 by Countyvise Limited, 1 & 3 Grove Road,
Rock Ferry, Birkenhead, Wirral, Merseyside L42 3XS.

Copyright      Irby WEA, 1991.
Photoset and printed by Birkenhead Press Limited, 1 & 3 Grove Road,
Rock Ferry, Birkenhead, Merseyside L42 3XS.

ISBN 0 907768 41 5

All rights reserved. No part of this publication may be reproduced, stored in a retrieval system, or transmitted, in any form, or by any means, electronic, chemical, mechanical, photocopying, recording or otherwise, without the prior permission of the publisher.

Wallasey. Later I went down to the South Coast to look after my husband's family in Bognor, and worked there as an Underground telephonist watching for planes to cross the coastline into England.

By 1942 I had been officially called-up and came back to home area, to be employed at Burton Manor, which was then a NAAFI Headquarters of Western Command, Chester. Our task was to buy and store large amounts of food for the forces and in case of invasion. Visiting my parents was difficult because of travel restrictions, and we spent our weekends 'on manoeuvres' with the local Home Guard and Volunteer Fire Service. This caused much hilarity, as our 'manoeuvres' consisted mainly of crawling along dusty hedgerows looking for suspicious people.

At home in West Kirby, neighbours formed fire-fighting teams, using stirrup-pump, bucket, sand and shovel on a long broom-handle. A white 'S' was painted on the garden gate of the house which possessed a stirrup-pump. Emergency water tanks, 12 foot square, were place on strategic roads for fire-fighting. Pigbins were placed on suitable corners for the collection of household waste to go to local farms as pigfood, and nothing was supposed to be wasted. Everyone had to carry his or her gas-mask at all times, in a cardboard box on a string around the neck. We practised using these at work at special drills — when a whistle was blown we had to immediately put them on and carry on with our work, even though the eerie noises coming from them as we breathed in and out were very strange. Special small ones were made for babies, which almost enclosed the poor child.

We occasionally visited the cinemas which were still open, in West Kirby at least. I helped in a services canteen some evenings, providing snacks and teas for airmen stationed at Newton, and the many soldiers who always seemed to be around.

My first child was born in 1944, in Brookfield Nursing Home, as the planes flew overhead practising for Arnhem — like a sky-train, with hundreds of gliders towed behind the planes.

The new baby had an extra Ration Book (green) and before the birth my allowance had been increased and I was given extra milk and vitamins. I had extra coupons for baby clothes and nappies and there was some knitting wool available. Things like maternity smocks and baby clothes were always passed on to others.

My sister-in-law kept rabbits, and we went to classes to learn how to look after them. We used the skins to make baby rugs and mittens etc. We also, of course, ate the meat. We learned to 'make do'.

*J. G. (Heswall).*

## Mrs Dorothy Smith

In 1939 I was a young lady in my early twenties, living with my mother, brother and sister in Aigburth, Liverpool; four miles from the city centre and near Otterspool Park and the River Mersey. This was a very vulnerable position as the river showed up clearly in night bombing raids.

At this time I worked in the Liverpool office of the Blue Funnel Line (Alfred Holt), now Ocean Fleet. Office jobs in the Blue Funnel Line were reserved for girls (most men had joined one of the services). Copies of manifests were sent to a store outside the city centre for safety, in case of bombing. During raids we all had to troop down to the shelters for safety, and there was unease in the office until all the staff were accounted for. Unfortunately some ships of the line were lost later in the war.

Travelling to the office was by tram at first although for convenience I bought a bicycle which I rode from Aigburth to the city centre, four miles away, by way of Sefton Park.

The fire raids of 1940 set Aigburth ablaze; among many other buildings burned and damaged by incendiaries were the Customs House, schools and our own house. We used to stick lace netting on to the glass to try to protect the windows. There was no siren heard for a bomb which completely destoyed Mossley Hill church in 1940.

My first voluntary work was giving out gas masks at Quarry Bank School in 1939. Later the Blue Funnel had a club for the many servicemen passing through the port, called the Angel Club. We office members were allowed to be late for work in order to serve breakfast to the servicemen.

In 1941 in the May Blitz the India Buildings were burnt-out, among many other Liverpool buildings. The Blue Funnel offices were evacuated to two large houses away from the city centre, the same buildings where the manifests were stored.

Rationing was endured by everyone and I remember enjoying a treat of fresh tomatoes. Queueing for shoes was a necessity.

I was married early in the war and followed my husband to various postings. My memories are of the wonderful spirit engendered by the hardships; everyone got on with their job as best they could. Life was full of frustration and goodbyes, and one was satisfied with very little. My memories are also of going to London, and Victory Day and the 1945 Elections.

*Gas-mask practise, 1940.*

## Mr G. Dutton, aged 25 in 1939.

When war started I had a job as a surveyor, but work was largely suspended at the outbreak of war, so until I entered the Army as a Specialist Observer, I helped my father in the family grocery business of Duttons in Chester. At the time my father was President of the Grocer's Federation of Great Britain and was very busy trying to organise the system of Rationing which had been brought in. At the start of rationing there had been a tremendous rush to buy and stock-up with goods, and large queues in the shop, but it was surprising how quickly housewives got the hang of it. One thing which would surprise us today was the large number of servants 'living-in' who also had their ration books as members of the household; these of course became fewer as the servants left to join the services or to go into war work.

When I joined the army I was sent to various training courses including ones at Blacon camp and at Formby where the food was recorded as being the worst in the army. My job included testing ranges of guns and entailed much travelling, so I billeted at all sorts of different camps. In 1940 I was stationed on the coast at Dover, where there was one rifle between ten men; we were told, in case of invasion, to pull a bough from the nearest tree and pretend it was a gun!

I was also watching the coast when the Battle of Britain started and I remember seeing literally hundreds of planes coming over. I was attached to the Highland Division and the initials H.D. once caused a spot of bother in a pub at Whalley in Lancashire, when a rather talkative Home Guard took it to mean 'Home Detail'; i.e. a soft job, or a malingerer. Nothing could be further from the truth, as I spent my war years travelling from one hot spot to another with not much rest. When I did come home for a spot of leave I stayed at my brother's house; he was in an Ack-Ack battery between Greasby and Meols, protecting the port of Liverpool (my parents' house in Chester had officers from Western Command billeted there). During my stay, Liverpool suffered an air-raid one night and, in the course of retaliation, one of the pieces of shrapnel from my brother's Ack-Ack gun smashed my bedroom window to pieces so I did not get much rest!

For some time I was working in Ireland and frequently travelled back to England, being besieged each time by female relatives to bring back pairs of nylons which were obtainable in Ireland. There was a lot of traffic in the Black Market; everyone used it. I remember one man at camp on Salisbury Plain who had smuggled back from

France a Magnum of Champagne. He had travelled with this all through France, carried it in the transport across the Channel, and was triumphantly bringing it into camp to show everyone when he tripped and fell, and the bottle smashed into pieces at his feet! The air was blue.

*Houses at Centurion Drive, Meols after bombing, 1941.*

## Mrs Dutton.

At the outbreak of war we had just returned from a summer holday. I have no clear recollection of the announcement on the wireless as I was teaching in the Sunday School that morning. The war did not alter my life very much, like others of my age group, just beginning our adult working life. I went about my daily routine as usual. My job with the Architect's Department at Crosville Bus Company was a reserved occupation. At the outbreak of war I was already doing a V.A.D. course with practical work in the local hospital; unfortunately with terminal cases. I feel I might have been more useful in another ward where I could have had experience of treating accidents etc.

Throughout the war I lived in Chester with my mother, grandmother and an elderly relative. At the beginning of the war Chester took evacuees from Liverpool and we had two schoolgirls billeted on us but these went back to Liverpool within three months. There were several training schools in Chester for people in munitions and several trainees stayed in our house. Our elderly relative also needed a home so we took her in; the only problem was that she saw no reason for the black-out restrictions as there had been none in the 1914-18 war, and this resulted in numerous brushes with the A.R.P.

I cannot remember much about food shortages, only queueing for tripe which was scarce. I worked on our allotment and grew some of our food, and my mother had been a dressmaker when young, so she was able to make clothes for us. I myself remember knitting a Fair-isle sweater out of bits of darning wool.

My social calender was varied; weekly evenings were taken up with youth club, rambling, badminton, Scottish or Olde-Tyme dancing, or working on the allotment. On Sundays I went to Church, helped with Sunday School or went rambling. Twice a week, on Thursday and Saturday evenings I helped at the YMCA canteen for soldiers at Eaton Hall, where there was dancing held at the soldier's recovery home. I feel I had much more social life due to the war and greater freedom than I should have had normally. What girl would want to cycle home alone at one o'clock in the morning these days? Another result of war-time conditions is that I appreciate what I have and take more care of things than the average teenager of today.

Chester was very little touched by the war. We heard bombers going over, but only two bombs fell on the city. We could enjoy the peace and freedom from air-raids and had everything to hand with the shops and theatres; in fact, we had the best of both town and country.

One amusing incident I remember was one day while we were all having lunch, the air-raid sirens sounded, we all moved under the stairs for safety, except Grandma who calmly sat there eating her stew wearing a metal washing-up bowl on her head.

## Miss Potter of Heswall.

Before war was declared, Miss Potter, as a local government employee, had prior knowledge of Civil Defence preparations; machinery for the setting-up of food offices and shelters etc., and the protection of buildings, so the outbreak of war came as no surprise. Private life and work continued as usual; even a holiday in France was taken just before war was declared, as war was, though possible, not thought probable.

At this time Miss Potter lived with her mother in Bebington, and worked in the Town Clerk's office. She remembers food rationing being introduced gradually. When fully enforced, rations were quite meagre, supplemented sometimes by food parcels from relatives abroad. There was official encouragement for families to keep a pig (or pigs), and official collection of foods scraps for pig swill. Food offices issued free 'Make-Do' leaflets of recipes, and there was a national scheme for the care of pregnant women and babies, in the form of extra rations, vitamin pills, orange juice and cod-liver-oil. There was also much black-marketeering in food.

When clothes rationing was introduced, 'off-coupon' material such as that used for black-out curtaining, also any old parachute cloth, was used where possible. It was considered patriotic not to look smart, and there were 'Make-Do and Mend' patterns for re-using good parts of old, worn clothing. Large families with not much money would sell some of their coupons (illegally of course!). Utility clothing (which carried the Utility mark) gave a certain standard of quality. Shoes were very scarce and later on were made with wooden soles because of the scarcity of leather. Stockings were mended and re-mended, as there were no nylons at the time.

Saturdays and Sundays were not always free because of shift-work, but were spent, where possible, in looking after the garden or shopping. During wartime people were more ready to put up with shortages and discomforts, and there was much camaraderie. Health suffered because of lack of sleep during bombing raids which were heavy and frequent at times, even though Bebington was some distance from Liverpool which was the main target for raids. Housing and living accommodation was scarce, and young married folk often had to live with in-laws, with consequent difficulties. Marriages were often delayed until after the war, also careers because of war service.

*Nurses salvaging blankets from a bomb-damaged Merseyside hospital.*

## A Child's Eye View.

At the outbreak of war my parents and I were living in Birmingham. We did not have a shelter in our garden but shared with Mr and Mrs Weaver next door. One night we had an alert and my auntie, who was with us at the time, jumped over a five-foot fence carrying me. Next morning she couldn't jump over two-foot-six.

At the time my favourite song for entertaining the people in the shelter was 'Bless 'em All', unfortunately my rendition went on 'the long and the shot, and the tall'.

Not long after, we moved to Worcester. Rarely were enemy aircraft seen flying low over the area but the first day we were there, my grandmother took me for a walk onto Pitchcroft (the race-course and river side) and the first thing she saw was a German aeroplane swooping over the field. The pilot wasn't interested in the inhabitants.

We heard planes overhead most nights but knew that there was no danger to us as they were always bound for the factories at Birmingham or Coventry. Soon we didn't even go outside to watch them go over.

Pitchcroft had a large area of grassland in the centre of the race-course which was ploughed up and turned into a cornfield.

Although we rarely saw an enemy plane at close quarters, there was one occasion when one flew over Lower Wick and saw what he thought was a camouflaged arms dump. In actual fact it was just a hump in the ground but he decided to drop a bomb or two which killed two milking cows, much to the farmer's disgust.

Before the war got really under way, we went to visit relations at Weymouth. The trains were all fitted with low-powered light bulbs, and it was difficult to tell where you were. The beach was covered with coiled, barbed wire and other anti-landing craft obstacles. Soldiers were on duty to prevent the public going on to the beach. One of the soldiers eventually relented and let the baby go on the beach (that was me).

I remember the men coming to collect the metal railings for the war effort.

My father was medically unfit for the forces and spent part of the war at the coal mines at Rugeley.

When the raids became more frequent throughout the country, it was a regular thing to see the bombers swooping across Weymouth Bay en-route for Bristol. Occasionally they had a bomb left on the return journey which they obligingly dropped in the Bay or the Backwater. The raid was known as the 6.15 special.

By 1942 the largest hotel on the promenade had been turned into a maternity hospital and my cousin was born there in April of that year. Later my auntie and cousin were evacuated to us in Worcester.

Periodically we would be told that the water was being turned off and my mother and auntie rushed to fill every bath, bucket and bowl they could find as no-one knew when it would be turned on again.

Later, when I went to school, all we seemed to see were convoys of lorries passing through on their way north. We were told that we must not shout to the soldiers 'got any gum chum', and were all very excited when one of the girls brought along a box of assorted chewing gum which had been thrown off one of the lorries.

Talking of things falling off lorries. One of my father's friends was making deliveries in the country when an American lorry passed-by going so fast that a carton fell off. Harry got out and picked it up. "What did you do with it Harry?" Dad asked. "I went after him", said Harry. "Funny thing though, I couldn't get the lorry to go faster than five miles an hour". The carton contained best salmon, a rare delicacy in those days. We got two tins, I think.

We had a few German prisoners-of-war who seemed to help the Parks and Gardens Department mainly. Very few people would have anything to do with them but Dad always spoke to them if he saw them and said they were very good workers. I remember coming upon Dad and two of them one day in the park. All three were doubled-up with laughter but I never did find out what the joke was. When they returned home, one of the men gave Dad a brooch he had made for me.

## George Rawsthorne.

At the outbreak of war, during the first week, there were celebrations that at last it had happened.

There were three immediate demands, for blackout material, torches (which were then partially covered with brown sticky-paper to restrict the beam) and shelters — Anderson outdoor shelters, and Morrison indoor shelters. At this time you were advised to dig your own trench in the garden. We still have a slight dip in one section of the garden where the trench was. Coarse net was also available to be stuck on windows to prevent glass splinters flying. Later sticky tape was stuck criss-cross fashion on windows.

With the rationing of petrol, two gallons per month for motorcycles and four gallons per month for a 10hp car, the public turned to the buses and trains for transport. Before 8 am a workman's return ticket from Thurstaston to Woodside cost 6d, and a return ticket from Irby to Woodside cost 5d. Workmens' train tickets were also available and they cost 4d return to James Street and 5d return to Central. In Liverpool there were no workmens' tickets on the trams and it cost 2d from the City to Edge Lane. The buses ran from Woodside until about 10 pm.

At the outbreak of war, I worked for Avery's Engraving firm situated near to the Crocodile Restaurant, at the back of Lord Street on the site now occupoied by the car park and the Holiday Inn. I was engaged on store and press advertisements. The job continued through the winter of 1939/40, but advertising generally, and the demand for illustrations, dropped. many of the men went into the forces, and about May 1940 the engraving business closed down.

Having failed my medical I looked for war work, and it was suggested by a friend that my talents were needed, and could be put to good use at the Automatic Telephone Manufacturing Co. in Edge Lane. At the interview I was asked what my wages were. The interviewer nearly fainted when he was told over £800 a year. He himself earned half that amount and had a staff of 1,200 to look after. I was offered £3 6s 0d per week with the promise of an increase when I was established in the job. The increase never came. The 'Auto' was the worst-paid war factory on Merseyside. By 1945, for a twelve-hour day from 8 am to 8 pm the wage had increased to £6 (for a six or seven-day week). The 'Auto' was engaged in making Giro compasses, auto pilots, communications equipment, radio and telephones and bomb releases etc. As this was essential war work it was possible to hold staff even if they were required for the forces. It

*Park Station, Birkenhead, destroyed by bombs, Spring 1941.*

was also impossible to move to better-paid jobs at the aircraft factories at Speke or Hawarden or the Royal Ordnance factories at Kirkby and Chorley.

In addition there was fire watching. The ARP Headquarters were on the King George V playing field. The ARP duties were: two nights duty at Irby, one night at home, then two nights "sleep-in" at the 'Auto' and two more nights at home.

Wirral was looked-upon as a risk area for invasion, and tank landing traps were placed along the Dee shores. The Home Guard guarded the estuary and beaches at night. An Ack-Ack camp was established at Thurstaston. The use of telescopes and binoculars was forbidden in the area — spies! Hilbre was out-of-bounds.

On the lighter side, there were dances twice a week in the Irby Village Hall to the music of a piano and accordian, played by Josie and her husband (from the Elm Stores) and the drums played by Fred Breznin. Dances were also held at Heatherfield Cafe and the Cottage Loaf.

The Irby Dramatic Society gave two productions a year in the Village Hall.

It was considered a great treat to have tea and cakes at Smith's, or tea and scones at Moore's cottage on Irby Mill Hill.

Almost everyone listened avidly to the radio. The 'Keep Fit' programmes in the morning were popular, and the radio doctor had a programme each day. Bebe Daniels, Ben Lyon, Vic Oliver, Tommy Handley and Jack Train and the I.T.M.A. team were all popular.

Everything was in short supply with rationing, and so everyone was encouraged to dig for victory to help out. Some people kept hens but for a lot of people dried eggs took the place of fresh. Sugar was used for jam-making and saccharine for beverages. Coal and fuel were in short supply. Only utility furniture, utility clothes and utility prams were available. Wallpaper and outdoor paint was unobtainable. Building materials were scarce and walpamur/distemper was the only paint available. Ingenuity in making things not readily available came to the fore and many an old 78 record was warmed and pressed into the shape of a vase or dish.

A canteen for servicemen was opened in the bowling pavilion, almost opposite the entrance to the Village Hall, and dances were held to provide funds for the food (special ration allowance). A supper cost 6d.

Before the war the subject of pregnancy was not discussed, but the secret could not be kept when the extra bottle of milk was delivered and a special ration book was issued. On one afternoon a week queues of expectant mothers could be seen at each stop along Thingwall Road, waiting for what was known as the 'Blunder-bus', to take them to the clinic.

One of the first bombs dropped in Great Britain fell in Irby on Sandy Lane. The Red Cross members collected funds from the sightseers who came to see the crater. The many unexploded anti-aircraft shells were a hazard.

On one occasion a German airman baled-out and landed in Heathbank Avenue. The women dashed off to make him a cup of tea while the men stood guard. Word went around that the 'parachutist had arrived' and the Home Guard turned out to deal with him.

In Liverpool, during the twelve nights of the May blitz, many people left the town to sleep in the fields. Later, with problems of unexploded bombs in the fields, people slept on the underground station platforms.

Walking to my parents home at Anfield along the side of the railway, from Edge Hill, I passed a goods train in the siding. I heard shells exploding and found I was passing an ammunition train which was on fire.

On another occasion while on fire-watching duty at work, I and my companions became aware of something tapping on the window. As it was forbidden to remove the blackout until morning, so we decided to wait until daylight to investigate further. When the time came and we uncovered the window we discovered a land mine, as big as a telephone kiosk, caught in the telephone wires and swaying gently to and fro against the window.

On the homeward journey after 8 pm, if you were on the bus from Birkenhead and the air-raid warning sounded, the bus immediately stopped and the passengers took cover in the shelter. After a while it was found, by regular travellers, to be more comfortable to lie down on the long rear seats and wait for the bus to continue when the 'all-clear' was sounded. The shelters were large underground affairs which had a night superintendent to patrol them. Even so, many illicit romances took place in them.

Irby had its share of evacuees. First from the Channel Islands and then from Liverpool. At different times we had a mother and daughter, and then a married couple who had been bombed-out in Liverpool, billeted on us.

There were very few cars on the roads of Irby. The doctor had an increased petrol allowance for his calls. The midwife rode a bike. Car and vehicle lights were covered with a metal disk with a four or five inch square centre front, with louvres on the front of the box.

Coopers of Liverpool made a weekly delivery of customers food to the Heatherfield cafe, which was then collected by the customers.

A grievance of the people in the cities and towns north of London was that the BBC always spoke of the raids on London and the South Coast but never mentioned the damage to the northern towns.

I couldn't help thinking of the school in Durning Road, Liverpool which received a direct hit. There were 400 people sheltering in the reinforced cellars. No survivors.

One man caught in the blast when Lewis's and Blacklers were hit was found wandering in a dazed condition well up Scotland Road, two or three minutes after the blast.

It was interesting to note that the shrapnel which fell on the local houses, bounced off the slate roofs but cracked the tiled roofs.

At one period, Levers' Holiday Camp (at Thurstaston) was used as a prisoner-of-war camp for prisoners working on the farms in the area. It was later used as a camp for Polish soldiers.

*"Still on guard", outside his bombed-out home after the October blitz, 1940.*

## Mr and Mrs Walter Bunn

When war started in 1939 I was 35, my wife Eileen was 25. We both lived in Liverpool, Eileen working at the Office of Customs and Excise and I at the Petroleum Board, hence my call-up deferment. I joined the ARP as a dispatch-rider and Eileen as a telephone operator. We were married in 1940 and on the eve of our wedding there was such a heavy bombing raid that we feared the ceremony might have to be postponed, but fortunately the wedding arrangements went ahead as planned.

After the wedding we went over to live in Bebington. In the May Blitz of 1941 my office in the Strand Building in Liverpool was burned-out and the company moved over to Wallasey. During the worst of the bombing we spent many nights with neighbours in the communal air-raid shelter, passing away the time playing cards and Monopoly in particular. One night a bomb dropped in our garden, uprooting trees and damaging part of the house, so that we had to be evacuated for a while. At this time Eileen left her job in Liverpool, taking a post in Lever Bros., in the time office; a good move as it was close to home.

We, with several of our neighbours, bought a pig which was housed at Claremont Farm, Clatterbridge. This necessitated me having to cycle to the farm every morning with swill to feed the pig before going to work at Wallasey. Sunday morning was mucking-out time at the stye, and the pig had to be scrubbed with a Dettol solution. The pig was eventually slaughtered at the abattoir, the local butcher cutting up the carcase. My wife and I, the farmer who had housed the pig, and the neighbours, shared the spoil, foregoing our bacon ration. I must add!

Later that year we managed to have a week's holiday, travelling by motorcycle and side-car to Little Stretton, Shropshire, and staying at a pub called The Green Dragon. Seemingly a bartering system existed there, with the local farmers supplying the publican with food and provisions while he in turn repaid them in ale. It worked well for us too, and at the end of the week there, we left for home with a goodly supply of butter, eggs and sugar, all of which were severely rationed at home on Wirral.

In 1942/43 living became more normal and we were able, on occasions, to have an evening's entertainment at the theatre. It was at this time that an American Transport Unit based itself at New Brighton, one of the GI's lodging in the house next door to my office. We became good friends and I was invited to visit him in the US. In 1943 Eileen and I arranged an excursion by train to York for the GI, for a sightseeing tour of the Minster and other places of interest. I remember we arrived at York at 5 o'clock in the morning and had to wake up my sister who lived there, at this unearthly hour. The ex-GI still visits us when he comes over to England, but we have not as yet taken up the long-standing invitation to visit America.

Before the war, in 1935, I had joined a motorcycle club; one of the members was a young German whose father and English mother lived in Liverpool. A motorcycle tour of Germany was arranged, and while over there, I noticed this chappie was extremely pro-German. I lost touch with him on our return to England, but strange to relate, in 1942 Eileen was waiting for a bus to go to work when this same German passed her (without acknowledging her, although he had known both of us well) riding a motorcycle. This happened several times. Eileen gave me the registration number of the bike, I was suspicious and called the police. Soon after, the police stopped the motorcycling German one morning and found he had no identity card. That was the last we saw of him, but later the police called and thanked us for our help in catching this 'suspicious character'.

About this time I joined the Home Guard in the Intelligence Section, and rose to fame as the loudest snorer in the unit, (but a few well-aimed boots soon put an end to that!)

*After a Merseyside air-raid, November 1940.*

## Mr V. Torrens

Mr Torrens was a young married man who was in the RAF, stationed near the docks for the first three years of the war. His wife lived at Crosby with his mother-in-law and children. The children were evacuated to North Wales and then to Preston a few months after the outbreak of war.

Food in the forces was quite plentiful but was poorly prepared and cooked, whereas the civilians were rationed quite severely. Clothes were also rationed for the civilians and children got extra coupons because they grew out of their clothes so quickly. While it was not easy to manage on the clothes ration, it was adequate, and there was a lot of make-do-and-mend.

As regards time-off, Mr Torrens had 24 hours off in every ten days, of course this was dependant on not being required for other things at the base or raids etc. Whenever he had time off, and his wife was also able to get time off, they went to visit the children, this wasn't specifically at weekends.

As regards the short-term effect of the war, one lived from day to day and hoped for the best, it was all a question of survival and improvisation and a longing for the end of it all.

The long-term effect of the war taught Mr Torrens a lot about human nature and gave him a wider outlook on the world in general, particularly with regard to the overseas service he did from 1942 onwards.

Warnings of air-raids and all-clear were completely out of phase with the arrival and departure of the raiders at the beginning of the war and people got so frustrated that they tended not to rely on them at all.

The first bombs of the war in this area were dropped on New Brighton, no doubt aiming for Liverpool or Birkenhead.

Mrs Torrens was in the ARP and before the steel helmets were issued she improvised with a colander to protect her head from the shrapnel. Small boys who were left in Liverpool collected bits of shrapnel as souvenirs and some had terrific hoards of it.

When people had to deal with incendiary bombs they used dustbin lids as protection and had buckets of sand at the ready. Mines were laid by aircraft coming down to water-level almost and depositing them. One of the ferry boats was sunk at the Seacombe landing stage and for several months it lay there with just its funnel showing above the water.

One day a barrage balloon came down on the shore at Seaforth. The balloon crew went to retrieve it and a raider dropped a bomb about 20/30 yards away which fortunately landed on the shore and created a large crater.

After a night of heavy bombing the air would be filled with smoke and ash which enveloped everyone, and several separate fires would be burning among the piles of debris.

Mr Torrens had a room in one of the houses which had been requisitioned by the RAF. One evening he hung his best jacket on the picture-rail at the rear of the room. He was subsequently called away for the night and on returning next morning after another raid, found that the blue dye used for blacking out the windows was all over his jacket, the windows having been blown-in by a land mine.

Most of the bombing was at night and only one or two isolated enemy planes came in the daytime. The blitz of Liverpool reached its height during the first eight days of May 1941. An amusing note to end on — Mr Torren's wife came home to Crosby after work one day and the sirens sounded, she rushed into the back garden and collected the washing off the line and then opened the back door and pushed the washing into the arms of a strange man — she had the wrong house!

## Mrs I. Barker (aged 6 when war was declared)

Early in 1939 gas masks had been issued, and I can remember hearing the news of the declaration of war on the wireless on Sunday, September 3rd. At that time I was six years old and lived with my parents and elder sister over my father's grocery shop in Bromborough.

Shortly after this the pupils at my school (Woodslee Primary) went part-time, either morning or afternoon, probably because of the lack of teachers, as by this time many male teachers were in the forces. A school meal service started soon afterwards, dinners being cooked in a central canteen for distribution in insulated containers to individual schools.

By the time I was ten years old I was counting and bundling tea coupons and points coupons for tinned meat and fruit, to help my father in the shop. Sometimes we managed to get tins of salmon to sell, and there was also American Spam widely used. Each person was issued with a Ration Book and then had to register with a grocer and a butcher. Ration Books lasted 12 months, and the meat ration was 1/4d-worth of meat per week per person (1/-'s worth of raw meat and 4d-worth of corned beef). Milk was also rationed, but families with children were allowed extra.

Clothing was also 'on coupons', and very difficult to obtain. Mercifully, my mother had kitted-out the family with new dresses and shoes etc, for a family wedding, a few days before the introduction of clothes rationing, and these things had to last. Afterwards, for the most part, I wore my sister's outgrown clothes. Things were so desperate on occasions that I remember my mother, after she had weighed out the flour into smaller bags, unpicked the pure linen sacks that the flour had come in, bleached out the printing, washed and dyed the material and made herself a dress.

In May 1941 I had to go into Birkenhead Children's Hospital with abscesses on my neck, which entailed two operations. This was at the time of the blitz in Birkenhead, and we were carried down to the basement shelter of the hospital during air-raids. One morning when we emerged from the shelter we found that all the windows on our ward had been blown-in. In those days parents were only allowed to visit their sick children once a week (Sunday afternoon).

In March 1941 came the first heavy bombing in our part of the country. A land-mine was dropped within 400 yards of the shop, the windows were blown-in, and remained boarded-up for the rest of the war.

My sister and I slept under the stairs during the heavy bombing, this being what my mother thought of as the safest place. My father was in the Civil Defence and spent his nights fire-watching. I remember my mother saying once that she didn't take her clothes off for seven days, since we had to be prepared to take cover in the shelter at a moment's notice when the siren went to warn of an approaching raid.

Weekends were busy for the family even though the shop was closed, as the weighing-up of groceries into 1lb and 1/4 lb packets as well as the books and paperwork for the shop had to be done at that time. But occasionally the family managed rambles to Raby Mere or Parkgate.

I grew-up during a time of war austerity, and was a teenager during the shortages immediately after the war, when pre-constituted eggs and dried milk were the order of the day. No real cream was ever seen, and later when I studied Domestic Economy, we had to use the most spartan of recipes. But although I had not known times of opulence, I think on the whole it did not do me any harm.

## A. G. (Wirral)

At the outbreak of war in 1939 I was 28, and working in a bank in Liverpool. I had digs, at first, in Wallasey — the recreation facilities were good there, with tennis and cricket clubs. The local cinemas were also of a high standard. The cricket club met regularly until a land-mine fell on the pitch, which put a stop to matches for a while.

My wife lived in West Kirby before our marriage, which took place just before the outbreak of war. At the time food was still available without restriction for the reception, and we even managed to get hold of a bottle of champagne to drink the health of the happy couple.

Before being called-up I did my share of fire-watching at the bank in Liverpool, and was also a member of the local Defence Volunteers. Only on one occasion did I go into a shelter and that was at Exchange Station the night the Custom House was hit.

My call-up came in 1942 and I entered the RAF, but was sent back to this area for twelve months. By this time Wallasey was proving a good target for enemy bombs so my wife returned to live with her family at West Kirby while I, having received my travel permit at last, was sent to Penarth and then Weston Super Mare on the Bristol Channel. Eventually I became an armourer, and postings followed at Kirkham in Lancashire, Hereford, and the furthest posting, to the Outer Hebrides.

While we were in Wallasey I remember the dock area being badly hit. During one night of bombing we lost all the windows in our house. The next morning sisalcraft was fitted, but that same night a time bomb landed further up the road, so the sisalcraft too was lost — back to square one! One thing which struck me particularly was that no matter how heavy and devastating the bombing had been, nature took over and the bombed areas were eventually being covered by wild flowers such as Yellow Tansy and Rosebay Willow Herb.

## Reg Bushell, Parkgate.

In 1939 I lived with my family on the Wirral shore of the River Dee at Parkgate, then a small quiet fishing village. My father, grandfather and myself, when I was not at school, worked the two family fishing boats on the Dee and fished from Gayton down to the Point of Ayr and Rhyl, catching codling, ray, plaice or shrimps according to the season of the year. As our house (the old Watch House) was right on the shore our lives were very much bound up with the life of the river, its twice-daily tides, the frequent storms or squalls which affected our daily life and livelihood, and the different vessels passing up and down the river.

During the war, most of the fish we caught was collected as we landed, to be taken in large lorries to Liverpool Fish Market to be rationed out to the fish shops. All food was scarce so our fish was an important source of protein. Full-time fishermen were allowed seamen's rations (more than ordinary civilians) and we were allocated extra fuel for our boat's diesel engines. Because most able-bodied fishermen had been called-up, and most large trawlers, together with their crews, had been conscripted as minesweepers, the Liverpool Bay area was not trawled for almost the whole period of the war, and fish were there in abundance for our smaller inshore boats.

My father was just 40 years old in 1939 and too old for call-up, although he had served all through the 1914-18 war on minesweepers in the Dardanelles, and had taken his Mate's ticket while in the Royal Navy. However, he had been a member of the Naval Reserve for m..ny years, so when Commander Brunning of the Admiralty Office in Liverpool was looking for someone with good local knowledge of the Dee to serve on an Examination Boat, to be based at Mostyn Dock, he contacted my father, who volunteered for the job.

The 'Apt' was a converted Fleetwood trawler, commandeered by the Admiralty to inspect all vessels entering the Liverpool Bay area. Two "Examination Officers", appointed by the Royal Navy, were on board to examine each ship's papers, and note its cargo, crew, and country of origin. This was to make sure no spies entered Britain by sea.

There were two Examination Boats based at Mostyn which shared watches, the 'Apt' and a much faster, twin-screw vessel, the 'Tamara'. There was also another examination vessel based out at the Liverpool Bar Ship.

*The Watch House, Parkgate, about 1948.*

My father served as mate on the 'Apt' and was in charge of the day-to-day running of the ship, navigating in local waters from the Point of Ayr right up to the Forts at New Brighton, off the North Wirral shore. These Forts were anti-aircraft gun emplacements built on wooden and concrete 'islands' and chained together in groups of four with ladders in between, like modern oil rigs. They were opposite Wallasey, New Brighton and Hoylake.

I remember one occasion in the last years of the war when I had left school and was fishing full-time in my father's boat 'Capella'. As we passed the New Brighton Forts the guns began shooting at German reconnaissance planes, and unexploded shells together with bits of shrapnel were dropping into the water all around us. "Get below deck out of the way" shouted my father, and I remember protesting indignantly that if a shell did hit us the thin wooden deck planks were hardly likely to offer much in the way of protection. So I stayed on deck to watch the aircraft swooping and turning over the water — for a teenage boy the war was an exciting time and we didn't think of the dangers.

As well as the Forts on the North Wirral coast, the Army had set up a line of decoys along the River Dee; wooden platforms above tide-level with beacons on top. The Army tended these, and built a series of bridges over the gutters to carry a railway line out to the platforms. When the air-raids started each night on Liverpool, the decoy fires were lit to make the bombers think it was the Liverpool docks, so they would drop their bombs on the marsh instead where no harm could be done.

There was a complete blackout everywhere; at night no lights could be seen on either side of the Dee, and all the lights were removed from bouys in the main channel. In the Welshmans Gut channel, towards the mouth of the estuary, groups of yellow bouys were used for daytime RAF practice, and the marsh area was used for training flights from Sealand Aerodrome, of Spitfires and Hurricanes. Some days the young pilots in these would swoop low over the fishing fleet as a joke, and on one occasion an aircraft actually hit the mast of the 'Capella', cutting it in two, and then had to roll over and over in the sky to rid himself of the bits of wood and steel wires from the mast. The next day an RAF officer came from Sealand, full of apologies to my father, with money to pay for a new mast.

The Parkgate fishing fleet, much depleted, carried on as normal throughout the war, crewed mainly by grandfathers and boys like me, not old enough for conscription.

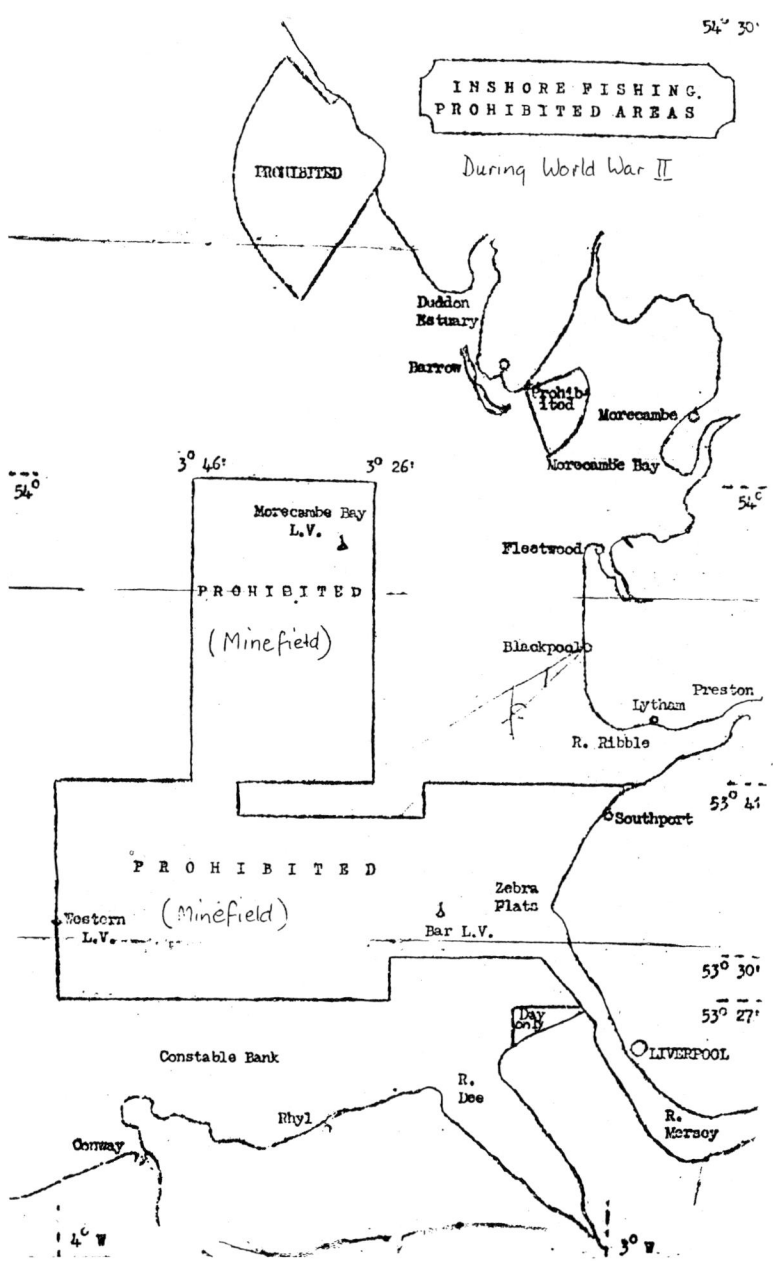

*Plan of prohibited areas, 1939-45. Issued to Dee fishermen, 1939*

A plan of prohibited areas was issued to all local fishermen, together with brightly coloured sets of international code signalling flags, a different letter of which was to be flown each week by each fishing boat, as a 'password'. Unfortunately most of the fishermen used these flags mainly to polish the engines, and they soon became a uniform, grubby black colour — thank goodness we were never challenged!

For my father on the Examination Vessel, things were much more organised. Numbers of boats intercepted varied; sometimes convoys could be seen off New Brighton of perhaps a hundred or more ships travelling in formation — destroyers on the outside, merchant ships in the centre — until they reached the Bar Ship, when they went singly up the Queen's Channel to the docks. Liverpool Docks were a hive of activity and an important target for German Raiders. Night after night we heard them coming over in the dark, looking for landmarks, lights, and the rivers shining in the moonlight.

Most nights the ironworks at Mostyn opened their furnaces at a certain time to release the slag and dross. The furnaces had to be 'tapped' at just the right temperature or the molten steel would be spoiled. This 'tapping' lit up the whole sky as the slag was removed, to be tipped on the shore alongside Mostyn Dock. Father reckoned that German bombers waited for this 'tipping' every night in order to take a bearing for Liverpool, before they set off to bomb the city.

My father stayed on the 'Apt' for some time, returning to Parkgate for his leaves. However, after the first few years of the war, the Examination Service was re-organised and run on a strictly official basis by the Royal Navy, using their own personnel. Father had the option of either staying with the ship and joining-up again as a regular seaman (which meant he could be sent anywhere at any time) or leaving the service completely. Having served through one war already, and now at 42 with a family to provide for, he decided to leave the Examination Service, and came back to Parkgate, and to fishing full-time.